ATTRACT SUCCESS

Unlock Your Inner Potential to Achieve Lasting Fulfillment

All Rights Reserved

Attract success Unlock Your Inner Potential to Achieve Lasting Fulfillment

© 2025 Zen Hunter

Published by Dofil Press

No part of this publication may be reproduced, distributed, stored in a retrieval system, or transmitted in any form or by any means, including electronic, mechanical, photocopying, recording, or otherwise, without the prior written permission of the author and publisher, except as permitted by law.

This book is provided for informational and educational purposes only. Although the author and publisher have made every effort to ensure the accuracy and completeness of information contained in this publication, they assume no responsibility for errors, inaccuracies, omissions, or any inconsistency herein. Readers are responsible for applying their own judgment and discretion.

All trademarks mentioned herein are the property of their respective owners.

For permissions, inquiries, or further information, please contact:

Dofil Press
Dofil.co.uk

First Edition, 2025

"Success doesn't chase people.

Success is attracted to the person you become."

Contents

Introduction   7

Chapter 1: Recognizing the Inner Blocks   11

Chapter 2: The Origins of Self-Doubt   15

Chapter 4: Embracing a Growth Mindset   23

Chapter 5: The Power of Visualization   29

Chapter 6: Aligning with Purpose   33

Chapter 7: Goal Setting and Planning   37

Chapter 8: Building Empowering Habits   41

Chapter 9: Overcoming Obstacles and Staying Motivated   45

Chapter 10: The Role of Relationships and Community   51

Chapter 11: Continuous Learning and Growth   55

Chapter 12: Giving Back and Creating Impact   59

Chapter 13: Mastering Emotional Intelligence   63

Chapter 14: Financial Mastery for Lasting Success   67

Chapter 15: Health, Energy & Peak Performance   73

Chapter 16: Creativity, Innovation & Continuous Reinvention   79

Chapter 17: Time Mastery & Peak Productivity   83

Chapter 18: Personal Branding & Authentic Influence   87

Chapter 19: Legacy & Long-Term Vision   91

Conclusion: 95

Introduction

The Journey Begins

Why This Book?

Success. We all want it. We chase it, dream about it, and sometimes spend our entire lives in pursuit of it. But success isn't just about wealth, fame, or achievement — it's about feeling fulfilled, waking up excited for the day ahead, and knowing deep down that you're living life on your terms.

I wrote this book because I believe that success is not something reserved for the lucky few. It's not about your background, where you were born, or how much talent you were given at birth. It's about tapping into something far more powerful — your **inner potential**.

The truth is, most people are not held back by their circumstances. They are held back by their mindset, their habits, and the stories they tell themselves about what's possible. This book is your invitation to challenge those stories, to break free from limitations, and to unlock the incredible success that already lives within you.

My Story and Why I Care

There was a time in my life when I felt stuck — like I was living on autopilot, doing the same things every day but getting nowhere closer to the life I wanted.

I thought success was something that happened to other people — those with better connections, more talent, or a head start I didn't have. I believed if I worked harder, if I just pushed through, eventually things would change. But no matter how much effort I put in, I felt like I was spinning my wheels. Success felt like this distant thing always out of reach.

What I didn't realize back then was that the biggest barrier wasn't outside of me — it was inside. It was my own mindset. My own limiting beliefs. The quiet voice in my head that kept saying, *"Who do you think you are?"* or *"You're not good enough."* I was waiting for permission, waiting for the right moment, waiting for some magic sign to tell me I was ready.

But the turning point came when I finally stopped waiting. Instead of focusing on what I lacked, I began asking different questions:

- What if success wasn't about waiting for the right conditions — but about creating them?
- What if my thoughts and habits were shaping my results more than anything else?
- What if I could train my mind the same way I could train my body?

That shift changed everything.

I started studying successful people — not just what they achieved, but *how* they thought, how they approached challenges, and the daily choices they made. I learned that success wasn't just about strategy. It was about mindset, clarity, and consistent action.

I stopped chasing perfection and started focusing on progress. I replaced negative self-talk with empowering questions. I built simple habits that compounded over time. And most importantly, I aligned my goals with my true values — not what others expected of me, but what genuinely lit me up inside.

This book is the guide I wish I had back then — a step-by-step path to unlocking your inner potential and achieving lasting fulfillment. My hope is that it will help you skip some of the frustration and confusion I went through, and give you the tools to create the success you deserve.

Because the truth is: **Success is not something you find. It's something you attract by the person you become.**

What You Will Learn

This book is not about hype or vague inspiration. It's about **practical tools and proven strategies** that will help you:

- Identify the invisible barriers holding you back.
- Shift from a fixed to a growth-oriented mindset.
- Set meaningful goals that align with your true purpose.
- Build habits that support your success — daily, not someday.
- Stay motivated through obstacles and setbacks.
- Cultivate relationships and environments that elevate your journey.
- Sustain long-term success and experience real fulfillment.

How to Use This Book

Think of this book as your **personal success roadmap**. Each chapter builds upon the last, guiding you step by step toward unlocking your fullest potential. Along the way, you'll find:

- **Reflection prompts** to help you apply the insights directly to your life.
- **Practical exercises** designed to turn ideas into action.
- **Real-life examples** to inspire and illustrate key concepts.

Don't just read this book — **engage with it**. Pause to reflect, answer the questions honestly, and most importantly, take action.

You already have what it takes to create a life you're proud of. This book is simply here to help you remember that — and to give you the tools to make it happen.

Now, let's begin the journey to attract success and achieve the lasting fulfillment you deserve.

Chapter 1

Recognizing the Inner Blocks

"I thought I was the only one who felt this way—like I was chained to my own doubts."— Sarah, startup founder

The Real Reason You're Not Where You Want to Be

If I asked you why you're not yet living the life you truly want, what would you say?
Not enough time? Not enough money? No connections? Wrong place, wrong timing?

These are the answers most people give — and on the surface, they make sense. But dig a little deeper, and you'll often find that the real barriers to success are not the external circumstances. They are the invisible, internal walls we build around ourselves. Walls made of fear, doubt, procrastination, and limiting beliefs.

The harsh truth is: **It's not the world that holds you back. It's the stories you believe about yourself.**

And the first step toward attracting success is becoming aware of those stories.

The Invisible Enemy: Limiting Beliefs

A limiting belief is a thought or assumption that you accept as true, even though it holds you back from reaching your full potential. These beliefs often sound like:

- *"I'm not good enough."*
- *"Success is for other people, not for someone like me."*
- *"I always mess things up."*
- *"I'm too old... or too young... or too inexperienced."*
- *"If I try, I'll probably fail — so why bother?"*

Most of these beliefs aren't even your own. They were planted in your mind by parents, teachers, society, or painful past experiences. Over time, they became the lens through which you view the world — filtering out possibilities and reinforcing a self-image that keeps you small.

But here's the thing: **Beliefs are not facts.** They are simply repeated thoughts. And anything that was learned can be unlearned.

Self-Sabotage: When Your Mind Works Against You

Have you ever caught yourself procrastinating on something you know could change your life?
Maybe it's applying for a new job, starting that business idea, or having a conversation that could move your relationships forward. You tell yourself, *"I'll do it tomorrow,"* but tomorrow never comes.

This is self-sabotage in action.

Self-sabotage happens when your subconscious mind doesn't believe you deserve success, so it creates behaviors that keep you stuck where you are — comfortable, but unfulfilled. It convinces you to stay safe instead of taking risks.

And the longer you stay in this cycle, the deeper the rut becomes.

The Comfort Zone Trap

Your comfort zone isn't just about physical comfort. It's about psychological safety. It's the familiar routines, habits, and thought patterns that require no courage, no vulnerability, and no stretch.

But nothing extraordinary grows in the comfort zone.

Success, growth, and fulfillment all live **just outside** of it — in the space where you feel uncertain, where there's a risk of failure, where you have to show up differently.

The mistake many people make is waiting until they "feel ready" to step outside that zone. But readiness rarely comes before action. In fact, it's the action that creates the readiness.

The Artist Who Couldn't Paint

Emily grew up loving art but was haunted by childhood comments: "You'll never be as good as your brother." As an adult, she bought every "Learn to Paint" book but never opened them. When a friend invited her to a beginner's workshop, Emily froze—"I'll embarrass myself."

A turning point came when she watched a video of kids fearlessly drawing outside the lines. She realized her belief—that only perfect art mattered—was robbing her of joy. She attended that workshop, painted clumsy flowers, and felt a rush of pride. Today, her "imperfect" pieces sell online, and she leads her own beginner classes.

Takeaway: Sometimes dismantling a belief means practicing the very thing you fear—then seeing the truth with new eyes.

Reflection: What's Holding You Back?

Before we move on, take a moment to reflect. Grab a notebook or journal and answer the following questions as honestly as you can:

1. What areas of your life do you feel stuck in right now?

2. What reasons (or excuses) do you usually give yourself for not taking action?

3. Can you identify any beliefs you might be carrying that limit your potential?

4. Where in your life are you playing small to avoid discomfort or failure?

5. What would change if you let go of those beliefs and acted as if success was inevitable?

Remember: **Awareness is the first step to change.** Once you can see the inner blocks clearly, they lose their power over you.

Chapter 2

The Origins of Self-Doubt

"I always thought my voice didn't matter—until I lost the chance to speak up and realized how much I had to offer."

— *Carlos, nonprofit director*

Why We Learn to Doubt Ourselves

No one is born doubting themselves.

If you've ever watched a small child learn to walk, you'll notice something incredible. They don't hesitate. They don't worry about falling. They simply try, fall, get back up, and try again. Failure doesn't discourage them — it's part of the process.

But somewhere along the way, something changes.

We stop believing that it's okay to fall.
We start fearing failure.
We begin to question whether we're good enough.
And that's where self-doubt is born.

Self-doubt doesn't appear out of thin air. It is planted, watered, and nurtured over time — through words we've heard, experiences we've lived, and expectations we've absorbed from the world around us.

To truly unlock your potential, you need to understand where your doubt comes from. Because what was learned can be unlearned.

The Seeds of Self-Doubt: Where It All Begins

1. Childhood Conditioning

Most of our beliefs about ourselves are formed early in life. As children, we're like sponges, absorbing everything we hear from parents, teachers, and authority figures.

- If you were constantly told *"You're so careless"* — you might have learned to believe that you're incapable.

- If you were compared to siblings or peers — you may have adopted the idea that you're not good enough.

- If your efforts were met with criticism instead of encouragement — you may have learned to fear making mistakes.

The brain, especially a child's brain, doesn't easily filter what's true from what's just someone's opinion. It accepts these messages as fact.

Without realizing it, these early messages become the foundation of your self-image.

2. Social Conditioning and Comparison

As we grow older, school, social media, and society at large continue to reinforce certain standards of success.

You're expected to look a certain way, achieve by a certain age, and follow a specific path. If you deviate from these standards, you may feel like you're behind or not enough.

Social media amplifies this problem. You see highlight reels of other people's lives — the promotions, the vacations, the perfect relationships — and you compare them to your behind-the-scenes reality.

Comparison fuels doubt.

But remember this: **You are comparing your rough draft to someone else's polished final version.**

3. Past Failures and Negative Experiences

Every failure leaves a mark — but it's not the failure itself that causes the damage. It's the meaning we attach to it.

- Did you fail at a business idea and tell yourself, *"I'm just not cut out for this"*?
- Did a relationship fall apart and convince you, *"I'm not lovable"*?
- Did you make a mistake at work and conclude, *"I'm incompetent"*?

Failures are meant to be lessons, not labels. But when we internalize failure as personal identity, self-doubt takes root.

4. Fear of Judgment

One of the strongest contributors to self-doubt is the fear of what others will think.

We hesitate to speak up, take risks, or show our true selves because we're afraid of criticism, rejection, or embarrassment. We become experts at playing it safe — not because we lack the ability, but because we fear being judged.

But here's the truth: **The people who are judging you aren't doing any better.** Those who criticize from the sidelines are rarely the ones in the arena.

When you allow the fear of judgment to shape your actions, you give away your power.

Your Mind's Defense Mechanism

Believe it or not, self-doubt is your brain's way of trying to keep you safe.

The brain's primary job is to protect you from pain — physical or emotional. Doubt steps in as a defense mechanism to prevent you from taking risks that might lead to failure or rejection.

But the same mechanism that keeps you safe also keeps you small.

If you never risk discomfort, you also never grow.

Reflection Exercise: Tracing the Roots of Your Doubt

Take out your journal or notebook and reflect on these questions:

1. Can you recall moments from childhood where you felt discouraged, compared, or criticized?
2. What specific beliefs did you form about yourself during those moments?
3. Have you experienced failures or setbacks that shaped your self-image?
4. How has the fear of judgment influenced your decisions?
5. If you could rewrite the story of those moments, what would you choose to believe instead?

The goal of this exercise is not to blame the past — but to understand it, so it no longer controls you.

Awareness is the first crack in the wall of self-doubt.

Chapter 3

The Cost of Inaction

"I sat in that cubicle for ten years, telling myself I'd start freelance writing 'one day.' When I finally looked at my life, I realized I'd traded freedom for security—and I hated my choices."

— *Tanya, freelance writer*

The Hidden Price You Pay for Staying Stuck

Imagine standing at a crossroads. One path leads toward growth, risk, and the possibility of success. The other leads to safety, comfort, and the familiar — but also to stagnation.

Most people don't consciously choose failure. They simply avoid action. They hesitate. They delay. They wait for the "right time." And in doing so, they stay exactly where they are.

But here's the truth most people don't want to face: **Inaction is not neutral. It has a cost.** A heavy one.

Every time you put off that important decision, every time you silence your voice, every time you play small to avoid discomfort — you're paying a price. The price is your potential. Your growth. Your fulfillment.

In this chapter, we're going to talk about what it really costs to stay stuck — not just financially, but emotionally, mentally, and spiritually.

The Emotional Toll: Regret and Resentment

One of the greatest regrets people share at the end of their lives isn't about things they did. It's about the things they didn't do.

- ☐ The business they never started.
- ☐ The dream they never chased.
- ☐ The words they never spoke.
- ☐ The chances they were too afraid to take.

Regret is the emotional tax of inaction. The "what if" that lingers. The silent grief for a life that could have been more.

It doesn't happen all at once. It builds quietly over time, like rust eating away at metal. One missed opportunity after another, until you wake up one day wondering how life passed you by.

But the good news is: **You can stop the buildup of regret at any moment. All it takes is one decision to act.**

The Mental Drain: Overthinking and Anxiety

When you avoid action, you don't avoid the problem — you amplify it.

Procrastination doesn't make the task disappear. It turns it into a source of anxiety. The longer you wait, the heavier it feels. And the more mental energy you waste spinning in circles, thinking about it, worrying about it, and beating yourself up for not doing it.

Inaction feeds overthinking. Overthinking feeds fear. Fear feeds more inaction. And the cycle continues.

The brain craves closure. When you take action — even small steps — you interrupt the cycle and free up mental space for creativity, clarity, and peace.

The Opportunity Cost: Doors That Never Open

Every day that you hesitate, you miss opportunities you may not even realize were there.

- ☐ The skills you could be building.
- ☐ The connections you could be making.
- ☐ The momentum you could be gaining.

Action creates opportunity. Action signals to the world that you're ready. But when you stay passive, you send the opposite signal — that you're not ready, that you're not interested, that you're not committed.

And the world responds accordingly.

What's worse is that sometimes, opportunity is time-sensitive. The door doesn't stay open forever.

The Spiritual Cost: Dimming Your Own Light

Beyond money, beyond achievement, the deepest cost of inaction is the spiritual one.

It's the quiet frustration of knowing you're capable of more, but not living up to it.

It's the disconnection between who you are today and who you know you could be.

It's the slow erosion of your confidence and your spirit when you repeatedly silence your own desires.

When you hold back your talents, your gifts, and your dreams, you rob not only yourself — but also the people who could be impacted by what you have to offer.

Your ideas, your voice, your contribution matter. The world doesn't need you to be perfect. It needs you to show up.

Reflection Exercise: What Has Inaction Cost You?

Answer these questions honestly:

1. What important actions have you been putting off?
2. What has it cost you emotionally, mentally, financially, or spiritually?
3. How has hesitation held you back from the life you want?
4. If you had acted earlier, where might you be now?
5. What is one step you could take today to break the pattern of inaction?

This exercise isn't meant to make you feel guilty. It's meant to wake you up. Because awareness leads to choice — and choice leads to change.

Chapter 4

Embracing a Growth Mindset

"When I bombed my first sales pitch, I thought I'd never recover. But reframing that moment changed my entire career."

— *Alex, startup founder*

The Belief That Changes Everything

What separates people who rise after failure from those who give up? What allows some to thrive in the face of setbacks while others crumble under the weight of challenge?

The answer is mindset.

Your mindset — the way you view yourself and your abilities — acts like the steering wheel of your life. It determines how you respond to problems, how much effort you put in, and how you handle both success and failure.

The good news? **Mindset is not fixed. It can be changed. And changing it changes everything.**

In this chapter, you'll learn what a growth mindset is, why it matters, and how to cultivate it so you can step fully into your potential.

Fixed Mindset vs. Growth Mindset

The concept of the *growth mindset* comes from the research of psychologist Carol Dweck. Through decades of study, she found that people generally hold one of two mindsets:

1. **Fixed Mindset**
    - Believes abilities and intelligence are set in stone.
    - Avoids challenges for fear of failure.
    - Sees effort as pointless if you're "not naturally good at it."
    - Takes failure as proof of personal inadequacy.
    - Feels threatened by the success of others.

2. **Growth Mindset**
    - Believes abilities can be developed through effort and learning.
    - Embraces challenges as opportunities to grow.
    - Sees effort as the path to mastery.
    - Views failure as feedback, not as a reflection of self-worth.
    - Finds inspiration in the success of others.

Here's the truth: **The person you are today is not the limit of who you can become.**

The difference between "I can't do this" and "I can't do this *yet*" is the difference between staying stuck and moving forward.

How a Growth Mindset Fuels Success

When you adopt a growth mindset, several powerful shifts happen:

- **You stop avoiding challenges and start seeking them out.** Challenge becomes your training ground, not something to fear.

- **You become resilient in the face of failure.**

Instead of asking, *"Why did I fail?"* you ask, *"What can I learn?"*

- **You focus on progress, not perfection.**
  Small daily improvements become more important than immediate results.

- **You free yourself from the need to compare.**
  Growth becomes your own personal journey, not a competition.

This mindset doesn't guarantee success overnight — but it guarantees that you keep showing up. And showing up consistently is how success is ultimately attracted.

Common Growth Mindset Myths

Before we go deeper, let's clear up a few misconceptions:

- **Myth 1: "Growth mindset means anyone can be anything."**
  Reality: A growth mindset doesn't mean ignoring your current skills or circumstances. It means recognizing that effort, learning, and persistence can significantly improve where you are now.

- **Myth 2: "It's just about thinking positive."**
  Reality: While optimism helps, a growth mindset is rooted in action. It's about taking ownership of your learning, not just hoping things will improve.

- **Myth 3: "Some people are just born with a growth mindset."**
  Reality: Mindsets are learned — which means they can be unlearned and replaced.

How to Cultivate a Growth Mindset

1. Reframe Your Self-Talk

Pay attention to the language you use with yourself. Fixed mindset phrases sound like:

- *"I'm just not good at this."*
- *"I always fail at this."*
- *"I'll never be able to…"*

Growth mindset phrases sound like:

- *"I'm still learning how to do this."*
- *"This is hard, but I can improve with practice."*
- *"Failure is feedback, not a dead end."*

Start catching your fixed mindset thoughts and intentionally replace them with growth-oriented language.

2. Focus on Learning Over Outcome

Ask yourself:

- *"What did I learn from this experience?"*
- *"What skills can I improve to do better next time?"*

Celebrate effort, not just results. Recognize and reward yourself for showing up, staying consistent, and pushing through discomfort.

3. Surround Yourself with Growth-Minded People

The people you spend time with influence your mindset.

Seek out mentors, peers, or communities where learning and personal development are encouraged. Choose environments that challenge you to grow, not ones that keep you comfortable.

4. Embrace the Power of "Yet"

Whenever you find yourself saying, *"I can't do this"* — add the word *"yet"* to the end of that sentence.

- *"I can't speak confidently in front of others... yet."*
- *"I don't understand how to manage my finances... yet."*

This simple word shifts your brain from conclusion to possibility.

Reflection Exercise: Shifting Your Mindset

Answer these questions in your journal:

1. Where in your life have you been operating from a fixed mindset?
2. How has this belief held you back from taking action or learning something new?
3. How can you reframe these thoughts into growth mindset statements?
4. What is one challenge you can choose to embrace this week as an opportunity to grow?

Chapter 5

The Power of Visualization

"Before every race, I close my eyes and run the course in my mind—mile for mile."

— Alyssa, Olympic marathoner

See It Before You Achieve It

Every great achievement begins twice — first in the mind, then in reality.

Think about the world's greatest athletes, entrepreneurs, artists, and leaders. Long before they stood on the podium, closed the deal, or finished the masterpiece, they saw themselves succeeding in their minds. They rehearsed the outcome mentally before it ever became physical.

This is the power of visualization.

Visualization is not wishful thinking. It's not daydreaming or simply hoping for the best. It's a proven mental practice that aligns your thoughts, emotions, and actions toward the achievement of your goals.

In this chapter, we'll explore how visualization works, why it's so effective, and how you can use it as a daily tool to unlock your potential and attract success.

Why Visualization Works

The human brain is an incredible tool — but it doesn't always distinguish between real experiences and vividly imagined ones.

When you visualize an action with enough clarity and emotion, your brain activates the same neural pathways as it would if you were actually performing the task. This is why Olympic athletes spend hours mentally rehearsing their performances — because the mind prepares the body for success.

Visualization helps in three powerful ways:

1. **Focus**: It clarifies exactly what you want, reducing distractions.
2. **Motivation**: It ignites passion and keeps your "why" front and center.
3. **Preparation**: It mentally conditions you to face obstacles and handle success.

In short, **what your mind rehearses, your body and actions begin to align with.**

The Science Behind Visualization

Studies in neuroscience have shown that mental imagery activates many of the same brain regions as actual physical performance. In one famous study, people who simply visualized practicing the piano improved their playing almost as much as those who physically practiced.

This demonstrates that the brain forms connections based on mental rehearsal, strengthening your ability to perform the task when the moment comes.

But it's not just about the brain. Visualization also impacts your emotional state. When you see yourself succeeding, you create a positive emotional experience — which reduces anxiety, increases confidence, and builds momentum.

Creating Effective Visualizations

For visualization to work, it needs to be **vivid, intentional, and consistent**. Here's how to do it effectively:

1. Get Clear on Your Goal

Be specific. Don't just say, *"I want to be successful."* Define what success looks like for you.

- Where are you?
- What are you doing?
- How do you feel?
- Who is with you?
- What's happening around you?

The more detailed your mental picture, the more powerful the visualization becomes.

2. Engage All Your Senses

Don't just see it — feel it, hear it, smell it, taste it.

If you're visualizing giving a powerful presentation:

- What does the room look like?
- What sounds do you hear? Applause? Your own voice, steady and confident?
- How does your body feel? Relaxed? Energized? Focused?
- What emotions are you experiencing? Pride? Excitement? Gratitude?

The brain responds strongly to multi-sensory experiences.

3. Add Emotion

Emotion is the glue that makes visualization stick. The more you can feel the joy, pride, relief, or gratitude associated with achieving your goal, the more your brain will lock onto that image.

Ask yourself: *How will I feel when I've achieved this?*

Feel that now — as if it's already true.

4. Rehearse Regularly

Consistency matters more than intensity. Spend just **5–10 minutes daily** visualizing your goal.

Choose a quiet time — early morning or before bed works well. Close your eyes, breathe deeply, and step into the mental movie of your success.

This is not a one-time practice. Make it part of your routine, like brushing your teeth.

5. Combine Visualization with Action

Visualization is a tool, not magic. While it prepares your mind, it still requires action to bring results into the real world.

Use visualization to keep your focus sharp and your motivation high — but follow it up with daily steps toward your goal.

Reflection Exercise: Visualizing Your Success

Set aside time today for this exercise:

1. Write down one specific goal you want to achieve.
2. Describe in vivid detail what success will look and feel like.
3. Spend 5–10 minutes visualizing this scenario in your mind.
4. Journal how you felt during the visualization. Did anything surprise you?
5. Identify one action you can take today to move closer to that vision.

Chapter 6

Aligning with Purpose

"My sales were fine, but I nearly quit—until I realized I wasn't selling software, I was freeing people from outdated processes."

— *Jordan, SaaS entrepreneur*

Why Purpose Matters More Than Goals

Goals give you direction. Purpose gives you fuel.

You can set goals all day long — earn more money, lose weight, start a business — but without a deeper "why" behind them, those goals often feel empty. Or worse, once achieved, they leave you asking, *"Is this all there is?"*

Purpose is what gives meaning to your actions. It's the anchor that keeps you grounded when things get hard and the compass that keeps you moving forward when motivation fades.

In this chapter, we're going to explore why aligning with your purpose is the key to attracting not just success, but **fulfilling success** — success that feels good on the inside, not just impressive on the outside.

The Danger of Chasing Goals Without Purpose

Have you ever hit a goal that you thought would make you happy — but instead, you felt… nothing?
Maybe you reached the income level, bought the car, got the promotion — but the satisfaction was short-lived.

That's what happens when your goals aren't tied to your purpose.

Goals are external. Purpose is internal.

When you chase goals without purpose, you risk spending your life climbing a ladder that's leaning against the wrong wall.

But when your goals are connected to your deeper "why," every step toward them feels meaningful. Even the hard days have purpose behind them.

What Is Purpose, Really?

Purpose isn't always some grand, world-changing mission. It doesn't have to be about saving the planet or curing disease.

At its core, **purpose is about contribution** — using your unique gifts, strengths, and passions in a way that serves something greater than just yourself.

It answers the question:

- *"How can I use who I am to make a difference — to my family, my community, my work, or the world?"*

Your purpose might be to inspire, to teach, to create, to build, to nurture, to innovate, or to lead. It may show up in your career, your relationships, or your creative pursuits.

The key is not how big your purpose looks to others — the key is how aligned it feels to you.

How to Find Your Purpose

If you're not sure what your purpose is yet, that's okay. Purpose isn't something you "find" as much as it's something you uncover through reflection and action.

Here are some guiding questions to help you discover it:

1. **What excites you?**
   What activities make you lose track of time? What lights you up inside?

2. **What frustrates you?**
   Sometimes your purpose is tied to the problems you most want to solve.

3. **What are you naturally good at?**
   What skills or talents do people often compliment you on?

4. **When do you feel most alive?**
   Think about the moments when you felt energized, connected, and fully engaged.

5. **Who do you want to help?**
   Is there a group of people, a cause, or a mission that you feel drawn toward?

Purpose often lives at the intersection of **what you love, what you're good at, and where you can make an impact**.

The Purpose Statement Exercise

To clarify your purpose, try completing this sentence:

"My purpose is to use my [strengths/skills] to [action/serve] so that [impact/outcome]."

Example:

- "My purpose is to use my creativity and communication skills to inspire others so that they believe in their own potential."

This statement isn't set in stone. It can evolve over time as you grow. But having even a rough version of your purpose helps align your goals with your heart.

Purpose Fuels Persistence

When your actions are tied to purpose, quitting becomes harder — not because you feel pressure, but because what you're doing truly matters to you.

Purpose keeps you steady through setbacks. It reminds you why you started. It makes the work worth doing even when no one is watching.

Purpose transforms success from just achieving goals into **fulfilling a mission.**

Reflection Exercise: Clarifying Your Purpose

Take time with these journal prompts:

1. What are three things you love doing so much that you would do them for free?
2. What causes, problems, or communities do you feel passionate about helping?
3. What strengths or talents do you bring to the table?
4. How can these passions and skills come together to serve others?
5. Write your personal purpose statement.

Remember: Purpose doesn't have to be perfect — it just has to be honest.

Chapter 7

Goal Setting and Planning

"I'd always set New Year's resolutions—lose weight, learn guitar—but by February I'd forgotten them. I needed a system, not just a wish."

— *Marcus, marketing consultant*

Turning Your Vision Into Action

Dreams inspire you.
Goals guide you.
Plans move you.

No matter how clear your vision or how strong your purpose, without action, they remain just ideas. Success is not built on wishful thinking — it's built on focused, consistent action.

But not all goals are created equal. Some goals motivate and energize you. Others overwhelm or confuse you. The difference lies in how they're set.

In this chapter, you'll learn how to transform your dreams into achievable, actionable steps — so your success becomes not just possible, but predictable.

Why Most People Fail at Goal Setting

It's not that people don't have goals. Most do.
The problem is that their goals are often:

- Too vague ("I want to be successful")

- Too big without clear steps ("I want to start a business")
- Focused only on outcomes, not processes ("I want to lose 20 pounds")
- Lacking emotional connection ("I think I should want this")

When goals are unclear or disconnected from purpose, they feel heavy. Over time, frustration replaces motivation.

But when your goals are well-designed and deeply aligned with your values, they act like a map — giving you both direction and momentum.

The Power of SMART Goals

A powerful framework for setting effective goals is the SMART method. SMART stands for:

- **S**pecific: Clear and well-defined.
- **M**easurable: Able to track progress and results.
- **A**chievable: Realistic and within your capacity, while still challenging.
- **R**elevant: Connected to your bigger purpose and priorities.
- **T**ime-bound: Set with a clear deadline or timeframe.

Example of a vague goal:
"I want to be healthier."

SMART version:
"I will walk 30 minutes, five days a week, for the next three months."

The clearer your goals, the easier they are to act on.

Break Big Goals Into Small Steps

Big goals can feel intimidating. But every big goal is just a series of small steps done consistently.

If your goal is to write a book, your steps might look like:

- Outline the chapters.
- Write 500 words per day.
- Edit one chapter per week.
- Hire an editor by a set date.

Small, specific actions build momentum. And momentum builds confidence.

Remember: **Consistency beats intensity.** One small step every day outperforms occasional bursts of effort.

The Power of Written Goals

Research has shown that people who write down their goals are significantly more likely to achieve them than those who don't.

Why? Because writing creates clarity and commitment. It forces you to move your ideas from vague thoughts into concrete action steps.

Action Step: Write down your top 3–5 goals for the next 90 days. Make them SMART.

Focus on Systems, Not Just Outcomes

Goals are about results. But systems are about processes.
The best way to hit your goals is to fall in love with the system that leads to them.

If your goal is to get fit, the system might be:

- Meal prepping every Sunday.

- ☐ Scheduling workouts into your calendar.
- ☐ Tracking your habits daily.

The outcome is the result of the system. Focus on the system, and the outcomes will follow naturally.

Anticipate Obstacles and Plan for Them

Success isn't about never facing obstacles — it's about being prepared for them.

Ask yourself:

- ☐ What challenges might I face on the way to this goal?
- ☐ What can I do now to reduce those risks?
- ☐ Who can support me when obstacles arise?

Having a plan for setbacks keeps you moving forward when things get tough.

Reflection Exercise: Designing Your Roadmap

Take some time to reflect and journal:

1. What are your top three goals for the next 90 days?
2. Are these goals SMART (Specific, Measurable, Achievable, Relevant, Time-bound)?
3. What small daily or weekly actions will move you toward these goals?
4. What obstacles might get in your way, and how will you handle them?
5. How will you track your progress?

Chapter 8

Building Empowering Habits

"I hit a wall every New Year—resolutions fading by February. Then I learned tiny habits mean big progress."

— *Nina, UX designer*

Success Is What You Do Daily

We often think success comes from big moments — the major breakthroughs, the lucky breaks, the once-in-a-lifetime opportunities.

But the truth is, success is built quietly. Not in the spotlight, but in the small choices you make every single day.

Your habits are the invisible architecture of your life. They shape your health, your wealth, your relationships, and your happiness. If your habits align with your goals and purpose, success becomes automatic. If they don't, no amount of willpower will save you.

In this chapter, you'll learn how to build the kinds of habits that support your success — habits that make progress inevitable.

Why Habits Matter More Than Motivation

Motivation is unreliable. Some days you feel like showing up, other days you don't.

But habits don't ask how you feel. They run on autopilot.

Once a habit is established, it requires less mental effort to maintain. You no longer need to decide whether or not to do the action — it becomes your default behavior.

This is why highly successful people focus on systems and routines, not just goals. Because habits do the heavy lifting when motivation fades.

The Habit Loop: How Habits Are Formed

Every habit works on a simple loop:

1. **Cue** – A trigger that tells your brain to start the behavior.
2. **Routine** – The behavior itself.
3. **Reward** – The benefit or satisfaction you get from completing the behavior.

Understanding this loop allows you to design habits intentionally.

Example:

- **Cue:** Morning alarm.
- **Routine:** 10-minute meditation.
- **Reward:** Calm, focused mind to start the day.

How to Build a New Habit Successfully

1. Start Small (Very Small)

The biggest mistake people make when starting new habits is going too big, too fast.

If your goal is to read more, don't start with *"Read an hour every day."*
Start with *"Read one page each day."*

Why? Because small actions are easy to stick to. And once you start, momentum takes over.

Remember: It's better to do something small consistently than something big inconsistently.

2. Make It Obvious

Design your environment to support your habits.

- Want to work out in the morning? Lay out your workout clothes the night before.
- Want to eat healthier? Put fruit on the counter and hide the junk food.
- Want to write daily? Keep your notebook or laptop where you can see it.

When good habits are easy to start, they're easier to sustain.

3. Attach New Habits to Existing Ones

This strategy is called **habit stacking**. You attach your new habit to a habit you already have.

Formula:
After I [current habit], I will [new habit].

Examples:

- After I brush my teeth, I will write down one thing I'm grateful for.
- After I pour my morning coffee, I will read one page of a book.

This creates a natural flow and makes it easier to remember your new habit.

4. Make It Satisfying

If a habit feels good, you're more likely to repeat it.

- ☐ Track your progress visually (like checking off days on a calendar).
- ☐ Celebrate small wins. Acknowledge your consistency.
- ☐ Reward yourself when you hit certain milestones.

Positive reinforcement makes your brain want to repeat the behavior.

Breaking Bad Habits

Bad habits follow the same loop as good ones. To break them, disrupt the loop:

- ☐ **Make the cue invisible.** (Remove triggers from your environment.)
- ☐ **Make the habit harder.** (Increase friction — for example, delete distracting apps.)
- ☐ **Replace the routine with a healthier one.** (Find a positive action to satisfy the same need.)

You don't eliminate bad habits by fighting them — you replace them with better ones.

Reflection Exercise: Your Habit Blueprint

Take a moment to reflect and journal:

1. What one new habit would have the biggest positive impact on your life right now?
2. What small version of this habit can you commit to daily?
3. What will be your cue or trigger to start this habit?
4. How will you make it satisfying and rewarding?
5. Are there any bad habits you'd like to replace? What positive habit could take its place?

Chapter 9

Overcoming Obstacles and Staying Motivated

"After my business launched, I hit my first $10K month—and then sales flatlined. I felt defeated until I learned to see plateaus as part of the journey."

— Elena, e-commerce founder

Success Is Not a Straight Line

If success were easy, everyone would have it.

The truth is, the road to achievement is never a smooth highway — it's a winding path filled with detours, setbacks, and unexpected challenges. You will face obstacles. You will have days when motivation feels far away.

But here's what separates those who succeed from those who don't: **they don't quit when things get hard.**

In this chapter, you'll learn how to navigate the inevitable obstacles on your journey, how to stay motivated even when your energy fades, and how to bounce back quickly when life throws you off track.

The Myth of Constant Motivation

One of the biggest myths in personal development is the idea that successful people are always motivated.

They're not.

What they've mastered is the ability to take action *even when they don't feel like it.*

Motivation is emotional — it comes and goes. Discipline and systems are what keep you moving when motivation is low.

So, instead of relying on motivation, build strategies that support consistency.

Common Obstacles on the Path to Success

1. Fear of Failure

Fear of failure can stop you before you even begin. But failure is not the opposite of success — it's part of the process.

Every successful person has failed more times than most people have tried.

Reframe failure as feedback. Ask yourself:

- *What is this experience teaching me?*
- *How can I adjust and improve next time?*

Failure is a stepping stone, not a dead end.

2. Procrastination and Perfectionism

Waiting for the "perfect time" is one of the fastest ways to stay stuck.

There is no perfect time. There is only right now.

Perfectionism often disguises itself as a virtue, but in reality, it's fear wearing a mask. It tells you, *"Don't start unless you can guarantee success."*

But action, not perfection, leads to progress.

Focus on **starting small and improving along the way.**

3. Negative Self-Talk

The way you talk to yourself matters.

- Fixed mindset: *"I can't handle this."*
- Growth mindset: *"I'm learning how to handle this."*

When obstacles appear, your self-talk will either empower you or defeat you.

Pay attention to your internal dialogue. Would you speak to a friend the way you speak to yourself? If not, it's time to change the conversation.

4. Distractions and Lack of Focus

In today's world, distraction is one of the biggest obstacles to achievement.

Your phone, social media, endless notifications — all competing for your attention.

Solution:

- Schedule focused, distraction-free time blocks.
- Turn off notifications during work periods.
- Use tools like timers or accountability partners to stay on track.

Remember: Focus is a superpower in a world of distraction.

How to Stay Motivated When the Excitement Fades

1. Reconnect to Your "Why"

When motivation drops, go back to your purpose. Why did you set this goal in the first place? What will achieving it mean for your life?

Purpose reignites passion.

Write down your "why" and keep it where you can see it daily.

2. Celebrate Small Wins

Progress fuels motivation.

Don't wait until the big goal is achieved to feel good. Celebrate every small step along the way.

Each small win reminds your brain that you're capable — and keeps you engaged.

3. Track Your Progress

What gets measured gets improved.

- Use journals, charts, or habit trackers to visually see your progress.
- Check in weekly: *What worked well? Where can I improve?*

Seeing growth, even in small increments, sustains your energy and focus.

4. Surround Yourself with Support

You don't have to do this alone.

- Find accountability partners.
- Join communities where people share similar goals.
- Seek mentors who can offer guidance and encouragement.

When your environment supports your success, staying motivated becomes easier.

5. Allow Rest and Recovery

Burnout kills motivation.

Success doesn't require constant hustle. It requires **balance**.

Schedule rest just like you schedule work. Recovery isn't laziness — it's part of high performance.

Reflection Exercise: Building Your Obstacle Plan

1. What obstacles have you faced in the past when pursuing goals?
2. How did you respond to those challenges?
3. What patterns of self-sabotage (like procrastination, perfectionism, or negative self-talk) show up for you?
4. What strategies will you use to overcome these challenges next time?
5. Who can support you when motivation is low?

Chapter 10
The Role of Relationships and Community

"After launching my first app, I thought I could do it all solo. Within months, burnout set in—until a fellow developer showed me the power of collaboration."

— *Devin, software entrepreneur*

Success Is a Team Sport

The myth of the "self-made" person is just that — a myth.

Every success story involves a network of people who contributed, inspired, challenged, or supported along the way. Behind every achievement, there are mentors, friends, partners, teachers, or even competitors who played a role in shaping the journey.

No matter how strong, smart, or talented you are, the people around you will either lift you higher or hold you back.

Success is not a solo mission. **It's a team sport.**

In this chapter, we'll explore how the right relationships and communities can fuel your growth, and how to intentionally design your environment for success.

You Become Who You Spend Time With

Jim Rohn famously said, *"You are the average of the five people you spend the most time with."*

Whether we realize it or not, we absorb the attitudes, beliefs, habits, and behaviors of those closest to us.

- Spend time with people who complain, blame, and make excuses — and you'll start doing the same.

- Spend time with people who take ownership, pursue growth, and push their limits — and you'll rise to meet that standard.

The question is: **Who's in your circle?**

The Power of Positive Relationships

Here's what strong, healthy relationships can do for your success:

1. **Encourage You During Setbacks**
   Good people remind you of your worth when you forget it yourself.

2. **Challenge You to Grow**
   The best relationships don't let you settle for mediocrity. They hold you accountable and call you to a higher standard.

3. **Provide New Perspectives**
   Fresh ideas, constructive feedback, and honest conversations help you see blind spots and find better solutions.

4. **Celebrate Your Wins**
   Success feels even sweeter when it's shared with people who genuinely root for you.

5. **Open Doors and Create Opportunities**
   The right connections can introduce you to resources, networks, and chances that you wouldn't find alone.

Who Do You Need in Your Success Circle?

Consider building your circle intentionally with these types of people:

- **Mentors** – Those ahead of you who can offer wisdom and

guidance.

- **Peers** – Friends or colleagues at your level who understand your challenges.
- **Supporters** – People who believe in you, encourage you, and cheer you on.
- **Challengers** – Those who push you to think bigger, act bolder, and stay honest with yourself.

Notice that one person doesn't have to play all these roles. Different relationships meet different needs.

The Danger of Toxic Relationships

Just as the right people lift you, the wrong people drain you.

Be mindful of:

- Chronic complainers.
- People who always play the victim.
- Those who belittle your dreams or discourage your growth.
- Friends who only show up when they need something, not when you do.

Toxic relationships don't just waste time — they sap energy, kill motivation, and can pull you away from your path.

It's not cruel to set boundaries. **It's necessary.**

How to Build a Supportive Community

If you don't currently have the kind of network that supports your success, here's how to start:

- **Join groups or communities related to your goals.** (Online forums, local meetups, mastermind groups, professional associations.)

- **Attend workshops, events, or classes where growth-minded people gather.**

- **Be the kind of person you want to attract.** Show up with integrity, give value, support others — and you'll draw similar people toward you.

- **Ask for help.** Don't be afraid to reach out, introduce yourself, or seek mentorship. Most successful people respect those who are willing to learn.

Reflection Exercise: Your Relationship Inventory

1. Who are the five people you spend the most time with?

2. Do these relationships support your growth or hold you back?

3. Are there mentors, peers, or communities you'd like to connect with?

4. Are there toxic relationships where you need to set firmer boundaries or create distance?

5. What actions can you take this week to strengthen your success circle?

Chapter 11
Continuous Learning and Growth

"I thought once I earned my certification I'd 'arrive.' But the industry evolved, and I nearly fell behind until I reignited my learning habit."

— *Dana, cybersecurity specialist*

Success Is a Journey, Not a Finish Line

One of the greatest dangers to long-term success is believing that once you've "made it," the work is done.

But true success isn't about reaching a destination. It's about **who you become along the way — and how you keep evolving once you get there.**

The most fulfilled, successful people aren't the ones who know everything. They're the ones who stay curious. They remain students of life.

In this chapter, you'll learn how to embrace lifelong learning as a key to sustained success, why growth never stops, and how to make learning part of your daily life.

The Growth Mindset, Revisited

In Chapter 4, we explored the power of a growth mindset — the belief that your abilities can improve with effort and learning.

Continuous learning is the living practice of that mindset.

It's choosing curiosity over certainty. Growth over comfort. Improvement over ego.

Because the moment you believe there's nothing left to learn, you close the door on your own potential.

Why Lifelong Learning Fuels Lasting Success

Here's why staying a student keeps you ahead:

1. **Adaptability:**
   The world is constantly changing. Those who keep learning stay flexible, while those who stop learning fall behind.

2. **Innovation:**
   New ideas come from connecting dots between things you've learned. The more you expose yourself to new knowledge, the more creative and resourceful you become.

3. **Resilience:**
   Learning helps you navigate uncertainty. When you know how to learn, you can face new challenges with confidence.

4. **Fulfillment:**
   Growth feels good. Progress — not perfection — is what brings long-term satisfaction.

How to Make Learning a Daily Habit

1. Read Every Day

Leaders are readers. But it's not about speed-reading or consuming tons of books — it's about **consistent engagement with valuable ideas.**

Start small:

- 10 pages a day.
- 15 minutes of focused reading.
- One new idea daily from books, articles, or podcasts.

Over time, this compounds into a wealth of knowledge.

2. Learn from Others

- Attend workshops or online courses.
- Join mastermind groups or professional communities.
- Seek out mentors who can share their experience.

Every conversation is an opportunity to learn — if you stay open and curious.

3. Ask Better Questions

Instead of trying to prove you know, ask:

- *"What can I learn from this?"*
- *"What am I missing?"*
- *"How can I improve this process?"*

Questions open doors that answers close.

4. Reflect Regularly

Reflection is learning's secret weapon. Without reflection, experience just becomes repetition.

Take time to ask yourself:

- *"What did I learn this week?"*
- *"What worked? What didn't? Why?"*
- *"What will I do differently next time?"*

This transforms mistakes into lessons and lessons into progress.

5. Teach What You Learn

Teaching forces you to organize your thoughts and deepen your understanding.

Whether you mentor others, share insights on social media, or explain concepts to a friend, **teaching is one of the fastest ways to solidify your own learning.**

The Danger of Comfort Zones

Growth happens at the edge of your comfort zone.

When you stop challenging yourself, you start coasting. And coasting always leads downhill.

Commit to trying new things:

- ☐ Learn a new skill unrelated to your profession.
- ☐ Travel to new places and engage with different cultures.
- ☐ Take on projects that stretch your abilities.

Stay uncomfortable. Stay growing.

Reflection Exercise: Your Learning Plan

1. What skill, topic, or area of knowledge would most help you grow right now?
2. How will you commit to learning it (books, courses, mentors, practice)?
3. What daily or weekly learning habit can you start immediately?
4. How will you track your learning progress?
5. Who could you teach or share your learnings with?

Chapter 12
Giving Back and Creating Impact

"When I volunteered to coach a local youth soccer team, I thought I'd be giving time. Instead, I gained leadership skills that transformed my career."

— *Derek, marketing director*

Success Is Best When Shared

There comes a point on every success journey when you realize something important:

The deepest fulfillment doesn't come from what you get — it comes from what you give.

Yes, success can bring freedom, security, and personal satisfaction. But the true legacy of your success is the impact you make on others. It's how your work, your time, your wisdom, and your presence contribute to the lives of people around you.

In this final chapter, we'll explore why giving back is not just an act of kindness — it's a critical part of a life well-lived. You'll learn how contribution amplifies your success, multiplies your meaning, and helps you leave a legacy that lasts long after the achievements fade.

The Fulfillment Gap

You can achieve your goals, earn the money, and hit all the milestones — but if your success stays only about you, it can start to feel hollow.

That's because we are wired for connection and contribution. We are meant to be part of something bigger than ourselves.

Psychologist Abraham Maslow, famous for the "Hierarchy of Needs," originally placed **self-actualization** at the top of the pyramid. But later in his life, he revised his view — adding **self-transcendence** above self-actualization.

Self-transcendence is the desire to go beyond personal success and make a meaningful difference in the world.

This is where the deepest joy and fulfillment live.

Why Giving Back Amplifies Success

Here's how contribution enhances your life and work:

1. **It Deepens Your Sense of Purpose**
   When your work helps others, every effort feels more meaningful.

2. **It Strengthens Your Community**
   Giving back supports the growth of others, which in turn enriches the environments you're part of.

3. **It Builds Relationships and Trust**
   Generosity creates goodwill. People are drawn to those who give without expectation.

4. **It Inspires Growth in Yourself**
   Teaching, mentoring, or helping others forces you to reflect, clarify your thinking, and continue learning.

5. **It Leaves a Lasting Legacy**
   Money and accolades fade, but the lives you touch create ripples that can last for generations.

Ways to Give Back and Create Impact

Giving back isn't limited to donating money — though financial contributions can be powerful. Here are various ways you can contribute:

- **Mentorship:** Share your knowledge and experience with those just starting their journey.
- **Volunteering:** Offer your time to causes or communities that matter to you.
- **Teaching:** Host workshops, write articles, or create content that educates and uplifts.
- **Donating Resources:** Support nonprofits, fund scholarships, or provide tools and materials where they're needed.
- **Everyday Acts of Service:** Small, daily acts of kindness — listening, encouraging, helping — create real impact too.

Contribution doesn't have to be grand to be meaningful. A small, consistent effort often makes the biggest difference.

Finding Your Way to Contribute

To discover how you can best give back, reflect on these questions:

1. What causes or communities do you feel passionate about?
2. What skills, resources, or experiences can you offer that would be valuable to others?
3. Who could benefit from what you've learned on your journey?
4. How can you give in a way that feels authentic and sustainable for you?

Reflection Exercise: Designing Your Impact Plan

1. Identify one way you can contribute your time, skills, or resources this month.

2. Set a simple, achievable goal for how you will give back.
3. Reflect on how contributing in this way aligns with your purpose.
4. Commit to revisiting your impact plan regularly — how can you expand your contribution as your success grows?

Final Thoughts: Success Is a Cycle

The more you give, the more you grow.
The more you grow, the more you can give.

Success is not the end of the story. It's the beginning of something bigger — the chance to uplift others, to inspire change, and to leave the world a little better than you found it.

As you continue on your journey, remember: **True success is not just what you achieve — it's what you help others achieve because of who you've become.**

Chapter 13
Mastering Emotional Intelligence

"I was technically brilliant, but my team hated my style. Once I learned to read the room, everything changed."
— *Rachel, software architect*

Why Emotional Intelligence Matters

Technical skills can get you hired—but EQ (emotional intelligence) determines how far you'll go. High EQ helps you manage stress, connect authentically, and lead with empathy. It's the secret ingredient behind enduring influence and fulfillment.

The Four Pillars of Emotional Intelligence

1. **Self-Awareness**
   The foundation: knowing your emotions, strengths, and triggers.

   - **Story:** Marcus, a finance director, noticed he snapped at colleagues before big presentations. By journaling his stress patterns, he discovered that last-minute prep always spiked his anxiety—and could mitigate it by adjusting his schedule.

2. **Self-Regulation**
   The art of managing impulses and moods.

   - **Case Study:** Lina, a marketing manager, felt panicked whenever a campaign underperformed, leading to hasty, blame-focused emails. She adopted a "24-hour pause" rule: draft responses, then review the next day. Mistakes dropped by 80% and team trust soared.

3. **Empathy**
   The ability to understand others' emotions and perspectives.

   - **Exercise:** Next time a peer seems off, ask two open questions—"How are you feeling about this project?" and "What's most challenging for you right now?" Notice their tone and body language. Simply being heard often shifts their outlook.

4. **Social Skills**
   Building rapport, managing conflict, and inspiring cooperation.

   - **Anecdote:** When Dev, a startup CEO, began ending every meeting by inviting "one new idea" from each participant, collaboration skyrocketed—and so did morale and retention.

Exercise: Your EQ Audit

For each pillar, rate yourself 1–10 and journal:

Pillar	Self-Rating	Example of Strength	Area to Improve
Self-Awareness			
Self-Regulation			
Empathy			
Social Skills			

Choose the lowest two and commit to targeted practice over the next month.

Building Self-Awareness: The "Emotional Log"

1. **Set Reminders** every two hours—pause and note your current emotion.

2. **Label It**: Joy, frustration, boredom, excitement, etc.

3. **Identify the Trigger**: What event or thought preceded it?
4. **Journal Insights**: Patterns reveal your hot buttons and passion drivers.

Self-Regulation Toolkit

- **Breath Breaks:** 4-7-8 breathing to reset your nervous system.
- **Physical Cues:** Tense and release your fists to defuse anger.
- **Reframing Prompt:** Turn "This is overwhelming" into "This is a chance to grow my capacity."

Practice one technique during your next stressful moment.

Empathy in Action

Case Study: From Manager to Mentor

After surveys showed her team felt unheard, Priya instituted weekly "listening circles"—15 minutes where each person speaks uninterrupted about wins and worries. Over six weeks, engagement scores rose by 25%, and solutions emerged organically.

Exercise: Host a mini "listening circle" with two colleagues. Take turns speaking for two minutes each—others simply listen and then summarize what they heard.

Enhancing Social Skills: The Feedback Framework

1. **Praise First:** "I appreciate how you…"
2. **Describe the Impact:** "When X happened, I felt…"
3. **Invite Dialogue:** "How can we handle this differently next time?"

Role-play this script with a friend or coach on a minor issue, then apply it to a real situation.

The "EQ Daily Check-In"

Every evening, spend five minutes asking:

- **What did I feel most strongly today?**
- **How did I respond?**
- **What would I do differently next time?**

Tracking these insights builds habits of reflection and growth.

Reflection Exercise: EQ Growth Plan

1. Which EQ pillar feels most "out of balance"?
2. What one daily practice will you adopt to strengthen it?
3. Who in your network can help you stay accountable?
4. How will you measure improvement in the next 30 days?

Chapter 14

Financial Mastery for Lasting Success

"I hit six figures in business and still felt trapped—until I realized my money habits were running me, not the other way around."
— *Jasmine, digital marketing consultant*

Why Financial Mastery Amplifies Your Freedom

Earning more income without solid financial systems often leads to stress, wasted opportunities, and stalled growth. True freedom comes when your money serves your goals rather than derailing them.

1. Building a Purpose-Driven Budget

A budget isn't a restriction—it's a design tool to align every pound or dollar with your priorities.

Story: The Creative Entrepreneur's Budget Makeover

Mia, a freelance illustrator, tracked her monthly income and expenses for the first time and discovered she was spending £400 a month on single-session coffees and subscriptions she barely used. She reallocated £200 toward a professional development fund and £200 toward an emergency cushion—giving her both skill growth and peace of mind.

Exercise: Your Purpose-Driven Budget Worksheet

1. **List Your Income Sources** (salary, side hustles, investments).

2. **Categorize Expenses** into Needs, Wants, and Growth (e.g.,

courses, mentorship).

3. **Allocate Percentages** – Aim for something like 50% Needs, 20% Wants, 20% Growth, 10% Savings/Emergency.

4. **Adjust & Implement** – Where can you reduce Wants to fund Growth or Savings?

2. Automating Your Savings & Investing

"Set and forget" rules out temptation and ensures consistency.

Case Study: From Impulse to Investment

- **Name:** Carlos, software engineer
- **Strategy:** He automated 10% of his income into a low-cost index fund each payday and 5% into an accessible "play fund" account for personal treats.
- **Outcome:** Over two years, his investments grew by 15%, while his "fun fund" kept him motivated to stick to the plan without feeling deprived.

Exercise: Automation Audit

1. **List Your Current Automations:** Savings transfers, investment contributions, bill payments.
2. **Identify Gaps:** Are any savings or investment goals still manual?
3. **Set Up New Automations:** Use your bank or fintech apps to automate transfers into:
    - Emergency Fund
    - Retirement/Long-Term Investments
    - Purpose-Driven Funds (e.g., courses, travel, major purchases)

3. Debt Management Strategies

Carrying high-interest debt is a silent success killer. A clear plan transforms debt from burden to stepping-stone.

Anecdote: The Snowball vs. Avalanche Debate

Sophie had £8,000 across three credit cards. Overwhelmed, she chose the "snowball" method—paying off the smallest balance first to build momentum. After clearing the £500 card in two months, her confidence soared, and she transitioned to the "avalanche" method—attacking the highest-interest balance next. Within 18 months, she was debt-free.

Exercise: Your Debt Repayment Plan

1. **List All Debts:** Include balances, interest rates, minimum payments.
2. **Choose a Strategy:** Snowball (smallest first) or Avalanche (highest interest first).
3. **Calculate Monthly Payment:** Allocate extra funds from your budget's Wants category.
4. **Track Progress:** Use a simple chart or app to celebrate each payoff milestone.

4. Diversifying Income Streams

Relying on one source of income is risky. Diversification builds resilience and accelerates wealth.

Case Study: The Teacher Turned Template Seller

- **Name:** Raj, secondary school teacher

- **Challenge:** Desired extra income without extra hours.
- **Solution:** He began designing and selling lesson-plan templates online. An initial weekend's work generated £300 a month passive income within six months.
- **Key Insight:** Leverage your skills into digital products or side services that require minimal ongoing effort.

Exercise: Income Stream Brainstorm

1. **List Your Top 3 Marketable Skills.**
2. **Brainstorm 5 Potential Side Hustles or Products** using those skills.
3. **Evaluate:** Which one aligns best with your time, resources, and purpose?
4. **Prototype:** Plan a simple pilot (e.g., one product listing, one service test).

5. Purpose-Driven Spending

Ensure your spending enriches your life and furthers your purpose, rather than distracts from it.

Deep Dive:

Before each purchase over £50, ask:

- **Why do I want this?**
- **How does it support my goals or well-being?**
- **What value will it add in six months?**

This pause prevents impulse buys and aligns expenses with long-term vision.

Bonus Framework: The Financial 4-Pillar Model

1. **Protection:** Emergency fund, insurance.
2. **Provision:** Budget for essentials (housing, food, transport).
3. **Progress:** Investments, skills, business reinvestment.
4. **Play:** Fun fund, experiences, treats.

Map your current finances onto these pillars to ensure balance and intentionality.

Reflection Exercise: Your Financial Mastery Roadmap

1. Which pillar needs the most attention right now?
2. What's one specific goal you can set for that pillar this quarter?
3. What habit or automation will support that goal?
4. How will you track and celebrate progress?

Chapter 15
Health, Energy & Peak Performance

"I was clocking 12-hour days but crashing by 3 p.m. I thought burnout was part of the grind—until I treated my health as a non-negotiable priority."
— Kendall, startup COO

Your Body: The Ultimate Success Engine

Kendall's endless hustle backfired: poor sleep, midday energy slumps, and irritability. When she switched to a performance-first regimen—prioritizing sleep, movement, and nutrition—her productivity soared, her mood stabilized, and she achieved more in eight hours than she had in twelve.

1. Sleep: The Foundation of Performance

Story: From Exhausted to Energized

Marcus, a freelance writer, survived on five hours' sleep, thinking it bought him extra writing time. Instead, he suffered writer's block and foggy thinking. When he committed to a 7–8-hour sleep window—using blackout curtains and a regular bedtime—his creativity and clarity returned dramatically.

Exercise: Your Sleep Audit

1. **Track:** Record your sleep and wake times for one week, plus perceived "energy rating" each morning (1–10).

2. **Identify Patterns:** Note bedtime habits (screens, caffeine, stress).

3. **Adjust:** Establish a consistent "power-down" ritual 60 minutes before bed (no screens, light stretching, reading).

4. **Evaluate:** After two weeks, compare your energy ratings and productivity.

2. Nutrition: Fuel That Sustains

"I thought quick grabs and caffeine kept me going. In reality, my blood sugar spikes and crashes were sabotaging my focus."
— *Priya, marketing consultant*

Case Study: The Balanced Plate Protocol

Priya began each day with a protein-rich breakfast (Greek yogurt, nuts, berries) and balanced lunches (lean protein + vegetables + healthy fats). She minimized refined sugars. Within a month, her mid-afternoon crashes disappeared, and her concentration improved by 30%.

Exercise: Build Your Balanced Plate

1. **Map Yesterday's Meals:** Write down everything you ate.

2. **Evaluate Balance:** Did each meal include protein, fiber, and healthy fats?

3. **Plan:** For the next three days, design one "balanced plate" each for breakfast, lunch, and dinner.

4. **Reflect:** Journal how your energy and mood respond.

3. Movement: Micro-Habits for Macro Gains

"I believed only hour-long workouts counted. Then I discovered that five-minute movement breaks every hour kept me sharp and pain-free."
— *Lena, UX designer*

Technique: The 5-Minute Mobility Break

Set an hourly timer. Every 60 minutes, stand and move for five minutes—walk, stretch, or do body-weight exercises. Over a workday, that's twenty-five minutes of movement that fights stiffness and boosts blood flow.

Exercise: Design Your Movement Flow

1. **List:** Three activities you enjoy (e.g., brisk walk, yoga sun salutes, desk push-ups).

2. **Schedule:** Assign one to each work break (morning, midday, afternoon).

3. **Track:** Note your adherence and any changes in posture, mood, or focus.

4. Stress Management: Building Your Recovery Toolbox

"I thought stress was the price of success—until I learned recovery techniques that supercharged my resilience."
— *Omar, product manager*

The "Attention Reset"

When you feel tension rising, pause and perform:

1. **Box Breathing (2 min):** Inhale 4 sec → hold 4 sec → exhale 4 sec → hold 4 sec.

2. **Grounding Check (1 min):** Name—5 things you see, 4 things you feel, 3 things you hear.

This rapid combo shifts you out of fight-or-flight into present focus.

5. Peak Performance Rituals

Morning Ritual Example

- ☐ **Hydrate:** 500 ml water with lemon.

- ☐ **Movement:** 3-minute sun salutations.
- ☐ **Mindset:** 5-minute visualization of the day's key outcomes.
- ☐ **Nutrition:** Protein-rich breakfast.

Evening Wind-Down

- ☐ **Digital Sunset:** No screens 60 min before bed.
- ☐ **Journal:** One win of the day + one lesson.
- ☐ **Relaxation:** 10 min of deep-tissue stretching or meditation.

Exercise: Craft Your Personal Performance Plan

1. **Select One Ritual:** Morning or evening.
2. **List 3 Components:** (e.g., hydrate, move, reflect)
3. **Schedule It Daily:** Block the time in your calendar.
4. **Assess Weekly:** Journal improvements in energy, mood, and output.

The "SAE" Model

- ☐ Sleep: Prioritize consistent, quality rest.
- ☐ Activity: Integrate short, frequent movement.
- ☐ Eat: Nourish with balanced, purpose-driven nutrition.

Use this triad as your daily health checklist—address at least two pillars fully each day.

Reflection Exercise: Your Health & Energy Audit

1. Which "SAE" pillar feels weakest for you?
2. What one change can you make today to strengthen it?
3. Who can support or join you in this change?
4. How will you track and celebrate small victories?

Chapter 16
Creativity, Innovation & Continuous Reinvention

"When my industry shifted overnight, I either needed to adapt—or be left behind. Reinvention became my survival—and growth—tool."
— Tara, media strategist

Why Reinvention Is Your Competitive Edge

Tara watched peers cling to outdated methods as digital platforms exploded. By experimenting with new formats—podcasts, live video, interactive articles—she not only preserved her relevance but doubled her audience. In a world that never stops changing, your ability to innovate and reinvent yourself is your greatest asset.

1. Cultivating a Creative Mindset

Story: The Accidental Innovator

James, an operations manager, faced chronic workflow bottlenecks. Frustrated by traditional "fixes," he held a "wild ideas" lunch—no judgment allowed. One off-the-wall suggestion led to a simple kanban board that slashed lead times by 40%. His willingness to suspend "this won't work" sparked real innovation.

Exercise: The "Yes, and..." Brainstorm

Pair up with a colleague or friend. One person offers any idea; the other responds, "Yes, and..." adding to it. Continue building for five minutes. Notice how this open, additive structure uncovers unexpected possibilities.

2. Idea Quotas & Cross-Pollination

"I set a daily goal: jot down five new ideas—no matter how absurd. Some were duds; a few became product pivots."
— *Nina, food-tech entrepreneur*

Technique: Idea Quota

Commit to generating a set number of ideas each day (e.g., five headlines, five product tweaks, five new services). Quantity breeds quality; the act of ideation trains your brain to spot opportunity.

Exercise: Cross-Pollination Map

1. **List Three Unrelated Domains** you're curious about (e.g., architecture, gaming, herbal medicine).

2. **Identify One Concept** from each (e.g., "modular design," "level progression," "adaptogenic herbs").

3. **Combine** two or more concepts to spark a novel idea for your field.

4. **Journal** the top three combinations and explore one in more depth this week.

3. Prototyping & Rapid Experimentation

Case Study: The 24-Hour MVP

A coaching client, Priya, dreamed of an online course but feared the tech. Instead of building a full platform, she created a single landing page with a paid "preview session." In 24 hours, she tested interest, validated pricing, and gathered feedback—then built the full program with confidence.

Exercise: Your Quick MVP Plan

1. **Define Your Core Promise:** What's the simplest version of

your offer?

2. **Choose a Test Format:** Poll, landing page, sample session, mock-up.
3. **Set a 48-Hour Deadline:** Launch, collect feedback, and decide next steps.
4. **Iterate:** Use insights to refine or pivot.

4. Embracing "Constructive Failure"

"I used to hide failures. Now I celebrate them—each one is a data point guiding me closer to success."
— *Elena, e-commerce founder*

Technique: Failure Post-Mortem

After every experiment, ask:

- ☐ **What went right?**
- ☐ **What went wrong?**
- ☐ **What will I change next time?**

Document these in a shared "Learning Log" to build institutional knowledge—your own and your team's.

The 3R Innovation Cycle

1. **Resist Routine:** Question "the way we've always done it."
2. **Rapid Test:** Prototype and gather feedback quickly.
3. **Refine or Release:** Scale what works; discard what doesn't.

Use this cycle weekly to keep ideas fresh and actionable.

5. Continuous Personal Reinvention

Your career and passions will evolve. Plan periodic "reinvention sprints":

Exercise: Your Reinvention Roadmap

1. **Assess Current Self:** List your core skills, interests, and strengths.

2. **Envision Future Self (12–18 months):** What new skills or roles excite you?

3. **Gap Analysis:** Identify two skills or experiences you need.

4. **Sprint Plan:** Outline a 30-day sprint (courses, projects, mentorship) to close one gap.

5. **Celebrate & Reflect:** At sprint end, evaluate growth and plan the next sprint.

Reflection Exercise: Innovation Check-In

1. When did you last consciously generate a "wild idea"?

2. What experiment—from any size—can you launch in the next 72 hours?

3. How will you capture learnings from success and failure alike?

4. Which pillar of the 3R Cycle will you apply first this week?

Chapter 17

Time Mastery & Peak Productivity

"I felt busy but never productive—until I realized I was chasing tasks, not outcomes."
— *Samira, UX researcher*

Why Mastering Time Is Non-Negotiable

Samira's calendar was full, yet her key projects lagged. By shifting from "doing more" to "doing what matters," she reclaimed 10 hours a week for high-impact work—and finally shipped her long-overdue portfolio redesign.

1. Focus on Outcomes, Not Hours

- **Story:** Alex, a graphic designer, used to measure success by hours billed. When he switched to project milestones (e.g., "first draft complete"), his creative output jumped 30%, and client satisfaction soared.

Exercise: Outcome Mapping

1. List your top 3 recurring responsibilities.
2. For each, define 2–3 clear outcomes (e.g., "publish 2 blog posts," "prototype new feature").
3. Block calendar time exclusively for those outcomes—no meetings allowed.

2. The Two-Minute Rule & Batch Processing

"If it takes under two minutes, I just do it. Everything else I batch—emails, calls, admin."
— *Ravi, startup COO*

- **Technique:**
    - **Two-Minute Rule** for quick tasks.
    - **Batching:** Group similar tasks and tackle them in a single focused session.

3. Deep Work & Shallow Work

Case Study: The Writer's Sanctuary

Maria scheduled two 90-minute "deep work" blocks each morning—phone on airplane mode, door closed. In those sessions, she wrote 1,000 words. By afternoon, she handled emails and calls (shallow work), finishing her next e-book draft in six weeks.

Exercise: Deep Work Audit

1. Identify your prime creative period (morning, afternoon, evening).
2. Schedule two uninterrupted blocks of 60–90 minutes for your highest-value work.
3. Track adherence and adjust rhythms over a month.

4. The Eisenhower Matrix

- **Urgent & Important:** Do now.
- **Important, Not Urgent:** Schedule.
- **Urgent, Not Important:** Delegate.

- ☐ **Neither:** Eliminate.

Exercise: Matrix Sorting

Grab your task list and categorize each item. Immediately act on "Do Now," schedule "Plan," delegate one task, and cross off at least one item.

The PACT Productivity Model

1. Priority—Choose ONE top task per day.
2. Action—Define the very next physical step.
3. Control—Set boundaries (time, place) to protect your focus.
4. Track—Review progress at day's end.

Implement PACT for 14 days and note the shift in output.

Reflection Exercise: Your Time Mastery Plan

1. What's your biggest time waster this week?
2. Which deep work blocks will you schedule next week?
3. How will you batch your shallow tasks?
4. What will you eliminate or delegate immediately?

Chapter 18
Personal Branding & Authentic Influence

Why Your Brand Is Your Professional Currency

"I was a top performer but invisible—until I started sharing my process online. Opportunities followed."
— *Theo, Software Engineer*

Theo spent years delivering exceptional code behind the scenes, yet his name never rose above the din of his organization. It wasn't until he began blogging about his development workflow—complete with challenges, failures, and breakthroughs—that recruiters, conference organizers, and potential collaborators took notice. By making his expertise visible, he transformed his personal brand into a form of currency that paid dividends in speaking fees, consulting engagements, and leadership roles.

1. Defining Your Unique Value Proposition (UVP)

Your UVP is the heartbeat of your brand: the distilled promise you make to your audience.

Story:
Elena, a financial analyst drowning in spreadsheets and jargon, realized that her real talent lay in translating numbers into clear, compelling narratives. She adopted the moniker **"The Data Translator"**, reshaping her LinkedIn profile, blog, and presentations around that single idea. Within months, she was invited to speak at industry events and landed high-value consulting projects simply because her brand spoke directly to decision-makers hungry for clarity.

Exercise: Craft Your UVP

1. **List 3 Core Strengths.**
2. **Identify 2 Audience Needs** you uniquely address.
3. **Compose Your UVP Sentence:**

    "I help [your audience] achieve [X] by leveraging [your strength]."

Example:

"I help marketing teams improve campaign ROI by translating complex analytics into clear, action-driven insights."

2. Content Strategy & Thought Leadership

"I committed to one LinkedIn post per week sharing a real-world lesson. My network grew by 500+ professionals in months."
— *David, Marketing Strategist*

David's breakthrough came when he chose consistency over perfection. Each week he posted a short story about a campaign that went sideways—and the lesson he extracted. He paired these with micro-tutorials: crisp, three-step tips that his peers could implement immediately. By inviting questions, responding to every comment, and genuinely engaging with his audience, he built a reputation as a generous expert—and his network exploded.

Technique: Your Thought-Leadership Toolkit

1. **Story-Driven Posts**
   Share a challenge you faced, how you tackled it, and the insight gained.

2. **Micro-Tutorials**
   Offer actionable, bite-sized tips (e.g., "Three quick ways to boost email open rates").

3. **Engagement Hooks**
   Ask a question at the end of each post and respond to every comment to foster conversation.

Exercise: 4-Week Content Calendar

Week	Theme	Topic Example
1	Personal Origin Story	What drove me to become "The Data Translator"
2	Case Study with Takeaway	How a failed forecast taught me agility
3	"How To" Tip in Your Expertise	Three steps to simplify complex reports
4	Network-Sourced Question & Answer	Answer "What's your biggest reporting hurdle?"

3. Networking with Authenticity

If content is your voice, networking is your bridge to new opportunities. Authentic outreach honors both your value and the other person's time.

Case Study: From Cold Email to Collaboration
Maya admired a leading UX researcher and sent a concise message offering to help compile user-testing data. She attached a brief analysis of one of their published studies. Two months later, they co-hosted a webinar—an opportunity born from genuine curiosity and a value-first mindset.

Exercise: 3-Step Outreach

1. **Research One Target Contact.**

2. **Send a Brief, Value-First Message:**

    "Hi [Name], I loved your recent article on X. I've done some related research—would you like a quick summary?"

3. **Follow Up with Insight or Resource:**
    One week later, share an article or tool that complements their work.

4. Consistency & Credibility

Trust is earned over time, and nothing builds trust faster than reliability.

Anecdote:
Ravi launched a monthly newsletter on the first of every month—without fail. Over the course of a year, subscribers came to expect his insights in their inbox. When he introduced a paid consulting package, they were first in line, because his consistent delivery had built deep credibility.

The Personal Brand Pyramid

Level	Focus	Example Activity
Foundation	UVP & Audience	Write your UVP and update your profile bio
Content	Thought Leadership	Publish weekly articles or posts
Engagement	Networking & Community Building	Host a monthly virtual meetup
Amplification	Partnerships & Collaborations	Co-create an event or joint offer

Map each of your next quarter's activities onto the pyramid levels to ensure balanced brand growth.

Reflection Exercise: Your Brand Growth Plan

1. **UVP Audit:** How well does your current bio or UVP capture your unique strengths?

2. **Content Commitment:** What type and frequency of content will you produce over the next month?

3. **Collaboration Targets:** Who will you reach out to for authentic collaboration?

4. **Pyramid Focus:** Which level of the Brand Pyramid needs the most attention right now?

By defining a compelling UVP, delivering consistent, value-driven content, networking with genuine intent, and building credibility through reliability, you transform your personal brand into the professional currency that unlocks opportunities. Your authentic influence awaits—now it's time to put these strategies into action.

Chapter 19
Legacy & Long-Term Vision

Why Thinking Beyond Today Matters

"I realized my daily grind wasn't enough—I wanted to know how I'd be remembered."
— *Nina, social entrepreneur*

1. Crafting Your 10-Year Vision

☐ **Exercise: Vision Statement**

1. Imagine yourself in 10 years—profession, impact, lifestyle.

2. Write a concise vision paragraph as if it's already true.

2. Backward Planning from Legacy Goals

Case Study: The Nonprofit Founder's Roadmap

After defining her vision of "empowering 1,000 girls to graduate STEM programs," Aisha worked backward, setting 10-year, 5-year, and 1-year milestones—fundraising targets, program launches, and partnerships.

Exercise: Milestone Mapping

1. List your 10-year legacy goal.

2. Define 3 major milestones (5-year, 3-year, 1-year).

3. Identify immediate next steps for Year 1.

3. Aligning Daily Actions with Your Legacy

"I check every task against my legacy vision—if it doesn't serve it, I question why I'm doing it."
— *Ethan, corporate trainer*

Exercise: Legacy Filter

For each major task this week, ask: "Does this bring me closer to my 1-year milestone?" If not, delegate, defer, or delete it.

4. Mentorship & Succession

> **Anecdote:** Leo mentored two junior team members—one became his business partner, ensuring his work would continue beyond his direct involvement.

Exercise: Succession Planning

1. Identify one skill or knowledge area you want to pass on.
2. Select a mentee and plan a quarterly learning session.
3. Document key processes to transfer institutional knowledge.

Bonus Framework: The Legacy Wheel

Wheel Spoke	Area of Impact	Example Metric
Professional	Innovations launched	Number of patents/products
Community	People served/mentored	Mentees trained
Financial	Funds raised or donated	Donation totals
Personal	Relationships deepened	Key relationships maintained

Plot your current contributions on the wheel to spot imbalances—and expand spokes that need more focus.

Reflection Exercise: Your Legacy Blueprint

1. What do you want to be remembered for?

2. Which spoke on the Legacy Wheel feels strongest? Weakest?

3. What's one action you'll take this month to enlarge a weaker spoke?

4. Who will you involve to help build and sustain your legacy?

Conclusion
Your Success Story Awaits

When I began writing this book, my hope was simple: to guide you toward recognizing that success isn't an accident of fate, nor a prize reserved for the chosen few. Success is a craft—a lifelong work, built brick by brick through the beliefs you choose, the habits you nourish, and the daily actions you commit to. As you reach these final pages, I want you to feel a quiet confidence: you already have what it takes. All this book has done is help you uncover and sharpen the tools that have always lived within you.

A Journey of Discovery

Think back to our first steps together:

- **Chapter 1 taught you** to shine a light on the hidden stories—those whispers of self-doubt and fear—that kept you small. By naming them, you began to strip away their power.

- **Chapter 2 showed** you how those doubts took root: childhood messages, comparisons, past failures, and the fear of judgment. Once you saw the origins, you could start to rewrite your narrative.

- **Chapter 3 revealed** the true price of inaction—how each delay piled regret, anxiety, and missed opportunities onto your life. Recognizing that cost sparked the courage to choose progress.

- **Chapters 4 and 5 deepened** your mindset and imagination: you learned to think in terms of growth, to reframe "I can't" into "Not yet," and to rehearse success in vivid, multi-sensory detail.

- **Chapter 6 aligned** your goals with your deepest "why," infusing every objective with meaning so your daily efforts would never feel hollow.

- **Chapters 7 and 8** transformed those aims into concrete plans and automated habits—small routines that, day after day, compound into extraordinary results.

- **Chapter 9 armed** you with resilience strategies—how to face fear, crush procrastination, and press on when motivation ebbed.

- **Chapter 10** wove relationships into your success fabric: mentors, peers, and supportive communities who lift you higher and keep you accountable.

- **Chapter 11** committed you to lifelong learning—curiosity as your compass, active experimentation as your guide.

- **Chapter 12** invited you to give back, showing how contribution not only serves others but expands your own sense of purpose and fulfillment.

- **Chapter 13** sharpened your emotional intelligence, teaching you to navigate your inner world and connect authentically with those around you.

- **Chapter 14** laid out financial mastery—budgeting with purpose, automating your wealth, vanquishing debt, and diversifying income to free your mind for bigger visions.

- **Chapter 15** optimized your most precious asset—your body and mind—through sleep, nutrition, movement, and stress-reset tools so you can perform at your best.

- **Chapter 16** stoked your creative fire, equipping you with idea-generation sprints, rapid prototyping practices, and a reinvention roadmap to keep you adaptable in a changing world.

Each chapter peeled back another layer of possibility, showing you not just **what** to do but **how** to think, feel, and act differently—day after day, step by step.

Two Truths to Carry Forward

Across every story and exercise, two themes shine brightest:

1. **Ownership Above All**
   Nothing shifts until you take full responsibility—for your thoughts, your habits, and your circumstances. Blame and excuses may offer fleeting comfort, but they steal your power to shape what comes next.

2. **Action, Even When Imperfect**
   Insight without implementation remains inertia. Small, brave actions—flawed though they may be—break old patterns, build new ones, and set in motion the momentum you need to transform your life.

Your Next Steps

Now, stand in this moment and ask yourself:

- **What one decision** will I make today—right now—to move forward?
- **Which habit or action** from these pages am I ready to bring into my daily routine?
- **How will I ensure** I don't drift—who will I tell, what system will I set up, what reminder will I place in sight?

Success isn't a single giant leap. It's the sum of countless small choices, made consistently. You don't need all the answers before you start; you only need to take the first step.

Your Success Story Is Ready to Be Written

There's no perfect roadmap—only **your** journey, with its unique turns, challenges, and triumphs. Some days you'll feel unstoppable; other days you'll question every step. Yet when you stay anchored in your purpose, embrace growth, give generously, and persist through setbacks, that journey naturally draws success toward you.

Success isn't about luck. It isn't about waiting for life to hand you the ideal circumstance. It's about **becoming** the person whose daily choices, beliefs, and actions magnetize the opportunities and achievements you desire. And the first blank page of your next chapter? It waits here, in your hands, ready for you to fill with intention, courage, and heart.

Beyond the Book: Next Moves

To keep building on this momentum, consider:

- **Joining a Mastermind or Accountability Group:** Engage with fellow travelers who challenge you, share insights, and keep you honest.

- **Finding or Becoming a Mentor:** Teach to deepen your mastery, and seek guidance to accelerate your growth.

- **Setting Quarterly Sprints:** Every three months, pick a new, purpose-aligned goal—apply these frameworks to sprint toward it, celebrate the wins, then chart the next.

A Final Reflection: Your Commitment Letter

Take a moment now. Write yourself a letter that declares:

- **What success looks like** in your life—beyond metrics.

- **Why this journey matters** to your heart and soul.

- **Which patterns you refuse** to let define you any longer.

- **How you will show up** every day as the architect of your future.

Keep that letter close—on your desk, in your journal, or as a digital note that pings you weekly. Let it be your north star.

www.ingramcontent.com/pod-product-compliance
Lightning Source LLC
Chambersburg PA
CBHW061233070526
44584CB00030B/4111